Higher
Information Systems

© Scottish Qualifications Authority

First exam published in 2005.
Published by Leckie & Leckie Ltd, 3rd Floor, 4 Queen Street, Edinburgh EH2 1JE
tel: 0131 220 6831 fax: 0131 225 9987 enquiries@leckieandleckie.co.uk www.leckieandleckie.co.uk

ISBN 978-1-84372-682-1

A CIP Catalogue record for this book is available from the British Library.

Leckie & Leckie is a division of Huveaux plc.

Leckie & Leckie is grateful to the copyright holders, as credited at the back of the book, for permission to use their material.
Every effort has been made to trace the copyright holders and to obtain their permission for the use of copyright material.
Leckie & Leckie will gladly receive information enabling them to rectify any error or omission in subsequent editions.

[BLANK PAGE]

X054/301

NATIONAL QUALIFICATIONS 2005	THURSDAY, 26 MAY 1.00 PM – 3.30PM	INFORMATION SYSTEMS HIGHER

Attempt **all** of Section I and **one** part of Section II.

Section I—Attempt **all** questions.

Section II—This section has three parts

        Part A—Computer Application Software
        Part B—Expert Systems
        Part C—Hypermedia

Choose **one** part and attempt **all** of the questions in this part.

Read all questions carefully.

Write your answers in the answer book provided. Do not write on the question paper.

Write as neatly as possible.

SCOTTISH
QUALIFICATIONS
AUTHORITY

©

[BLANK PAGE]

SECTION I

Attempt ALL questions in this section.

Marks

1. Hilltown Sports Centre has a number of facilities available for booking including a swimming pool, 3 games halls, 3 Astroturf pitches and a climbing wall. Local teams can make regular bookings for these facilities at the start of each season. These bookings must be on the same day and at the same time every week.

   One example of Team Details and two examples of Facility Booking Details are shown below.

Team Details

Team Name	Broomhill Bullets
Sport	Basketball
Coach Name	Alison Hughes
Coach Contact No.	01265 777123
Day	Tuesday
Time	5–7 pm

Facility Booking Details

Facility Name	**Cost per hour**	**Capacity**	
Games Hall 1	£10	250	

Team Name	**Date**	**Payment Method**	**Duty Staff**
Broomhill Bullets	07/06/05	Cheque	A Young
Firrhill Fliers	10/06/05	Direct Debit	D Graham
Westfield	11/06/05	Cash	A Young

Facility Name	**Cost per hour**	**Capacity**	
Games Hall 2	£20	600	

Team Name	**Date**	**Payment Method**	**Duty Staff**
Cranford Colts	08/06/05	Cash	F Hardie
Broomhill Bullets	21/06/05	Cheque	R Lawson
Duthie Park Thistle	22/06/05	Direct Debit	R Lawson
Renfield Rangers	03/07/05	Direct Debit	D Graham

   (a) Identify the entities and their component data items in the existing system.   2

   (b) Convert the information in Facility Booking Details to first normal form.   2

   (c) State the primary key and any foreign keys for all **three** entities (including the Team Details entity) after normalisation.   4

   (d) Create an entity relationship diagram to show the relationships that exist between all **three** entities.   2

Marks

SECTION I (continued)

2. Neil and Gail both visited Toronto in 2004. Gail booked her flight through a travel agent and two weeks before her departure date, her ticket arrived by post. Her ticket is shown below.

AEROFLIGHT AIRLINES

From:	EDI	**To:**	YYZ
Date:	06/07/04		
Departure Time:	12.15	**Arrival Time:**	14.15
Flight No:	AFT653		
Passenger Name:	Gail Buchan		
Baggage Allowance:	20 kg		

*You must check in at least 2 hours before departure

767HK9003

(a) Define the terms *data* and *information* using examples from the ticket shown above to illustrate your answer.　　2

(b) The information on this ticket can be used for *planning* and *control*.

　(i) Give **one** example, from the ticket shown above, of information which would be used for planning. Justify your answer.　　2

　(ii) Give **one** example, from the ticket shown above, of information which would be used for control. Justify your answer　　2

Marks

2. (continued)

(c) Neil booked his flight on-line. Instead of receiving a ticket, he received his confirmation on screen as shown below. State the medium used to transmit:

(i) Gail's flight information;

(ii) Neil's flight information.

2

www.flyticketless.com

Flight Booking Details

Your details

Mr Neil Anwar

Your journey details

Your booking reference number is: **K3526726**

Leaving from **Edinburgh** on **Wednesday 7 April 2004** at **1:15pm**

arriving at **Toronto** at **3:30pm** (local time)

Total journey time: 7 hrs 15 mins

Your flight number is: **AFP670**

Your baggage allowance is: **20 kg**
Please note that you will be charged for any additional baggage over the allowance. <u>Click here</u> for more details.

Total cost: **£142**

> **Please remember to quote your reference number at the check-in desk. You must check in at least 2 hours before departure.**

*Please note you will not be issued with a ticket.

Thank you for booking with flyticketless.com.
Enjoy your flight

(d) Describe how the transmission medium used affects the accessibility of the information in both cases.

2

(10)

[Turn over

Marks

SECTION I (continued)

3. Strathmore Pony Club is preparing to implement a database of members and ponies. The ponies are available for hire and each one has a different hire fee. No hire fee can be more than £50. The club is currently at the stage of designing the database.

   Here are examples of the data held by the Pony Club.

Member ID	PG6754
Member Name	H Jamieson
Address	78 Seacliff Way
Town	Portsmouth
Telephone	01999 764222
Membership Fee	£75

Pony Name	Jelly Bean
Height (hands)	12
Gender	Male
Stall	3
Hire Fee	£30

Member ID	DL8744
Member Name	P Hammond
Address	152 Harbour Road
Town	Portsmouth
Telephone	01999 894362
Membership Fee	£100

Pony Name	Snowball
Height (hands)	6
Gender	Female
Stall	2
Hire Fee	£20

   (a) The Pony Club has constructed the grid below to show some of the characteristics of the data items associated with each pony. Copy and complete this grid by entering the data type and most appropriate validity check for each attribute.

   3

   Pony Details

Attribute	Data Type	Validity Check
Pony Name		
Gender		
Hire Fee		

   (b) The membership fee could be stored as either a text or numeric data type. One advantage of storing the value as a numeric data type is that it may require less storage. Give **two** other reasons why a numeric data type is preferred.

   2

Marks

3. (continued)

(*c*) Strathmore Pony Club offers courses in horse riding. At present it records information about its current riders, trainers and the courses it offers. The data is arranged in entities and attributes as shown below. The primary keys are underlined.

Rider
Rider ID
Rider Name

Course Booking
Course ID
Course Name
Trainer
Rider ID*

A database is created based on these entities and attributes. The tables below show the data entered into the database.

Rider ID	Rider Name
0356	H Kelvin
0184	P Robertson
0764	F Yates
1755	L Girvan
1844	T Whitehouse
1992	S Carmichael

Course ID	Course Name	Trainer	Rider ID
TK01	Trekking for Beginners	J Davidson	0184
TK01	Trekking for Beginners	J Davidson	0764
TK01	Trekking for Beginners	J Davidson	1844
TK02	Trekking for Intermediates	G Jacobson	0356
TK02	Trekking for Intermediates	G Jacobson	1755
TK03	Trekking for Experts	W Rogers	1992
SAH	Safety and Horses	P Watson	0184
SAH	Safety and Horses	P Watson	0356
SAH	Safety and Horses	P Watson	0764
SAH	Safety and Horses	P Watson	1755
SAH	Safety and Horses	P Watson	1844
SAH	Safety and Horses	P Watson	1992

What are the implications in the implemented database if the following amendments are carried out?

  (i) J Davidson, trainer for Trekking for Beginners, leaves and is replaced by A Walsh.

  (ii) D Dickson arrives as trainer for Horse Jumping.

  (iii) Rider S Carmichael leaves the Pony Club.

3

(*d*) Strathmore Pony Club is using a relational database to store its data. Describe **two** features that distinguish a relational database from a flat file database.

2

Marks

SECTION I (continued)

4. Students at Bayfield High School are entering a national multimedia competition open to all second year students. They have to create a multimedia presentation of no more than 20 slides on a topic of their choice.

   Each entrant has to complete the pro-forma below as they progress with the presentation. One of the students has decided to do her presentation on the band China Cats. Part of the pro-forma is shown below.

Daily Times
Multimedia Presentation Competition
Closing Date: 1 May 2005

Name: *Molly Weir*

School: *Bayfield High School*

Class: *2A*

Title: *China Cats*

Information Source	Information Selected
China Cats Concert Programme July 2004	1. Tour Venues 2004 2. Background information 3. Picture of album cover
China Cats Christmas Annual 2004	1. Photograph of band 2. Hits of 2003 and 2004 3. Details of band members

---

(a) Information can be classified as *strategic*, *tactical* or *operational*. The closing date of the competition is an example of strategic information.

   (i) Give **two** reasons why this information can be classed as strategic. 2

   (ii) Suggest **one** example of information from the pro-forma which could be classed as operational. Give a reason for your answer. 1

Marks

4. (continued)

(b) To find information on the band China Cats from the World Wide Web, Molly can use a search engine or a subject directory as shown below.

China +Cats –Country –Pets	**Search**

Arts & Humanities
Literature, Photography ...

Business & Economy
Finance, Shopping, Jobs ...

Computers & Internet
Internet, WWW, Software, Games ...

Education
College and University ...

Entertainment
Pop Music, Bands, Movies ...

When she used the search engine, Molly typed in the following query:

China +Cats –Country –Pets

The search returned 227,000 results most of which did not relate to the band.

(i) Explain why this search has resulted in such a large number of results which do not relate to the band, China Cats.   1

(ii) Make **two** changes to the search query which will reduce the number of irrelevant results.   2

(iii) Describe **one** advantage and **one** disadvantage of using a subject directory to locate information on the band, China Cats.   2

(c) Molly would like to include a China Cats music clip in her presentation. Comment on the legality of doing this.   2

(10)

(40)

[END OF SECTION I]

[Turn over

[BLANK PAGE]

SECTION II

Section II—This section has three parts

Choose **one** part and attempt **all** of the questions in this part.

[Turn over

Part A—Computer Application Software

Attempt ALL questions in this part.

Marks

5. LiveWell is a small company which employs staff trained in the use of four types of application software, namely *word processing*, *financial*, *spreadsheet* and *communication*.

   (a) As part of its development programme, the company wishes to train staff in further types of application software.

   State **four** further types of application software.   2

   (b) The financial software no longer meets the needs of LiveWell. It is therefore considering whether to upgrade to the latest version of the existing financial software or replace it with an alternative financial software package. It will be cheaper for the company to upgrade the software rather than replace it.

     (i) In order to reach a decision, how would LiveWell compare the two options in terms of

       • *functionality* and
       • *ease of use*.   2

     (ii) Describe **three** key hardware factors that could also influence their decision.   3

   (c) LiveWell decides to purchase and install the alternative financial software package.

     (i) Describe **two** customisations that could be made during installation.   2

     (ii) Describe **one** customisation that individual users could make to the software after it has been installed.   1

   (10)

Marks

Part A—Computer Application Software (continued)

6. Alistair has purchased a new word processing package. He has been experimenting with some of the features of the package and discovers that he can insert graphics into documents.

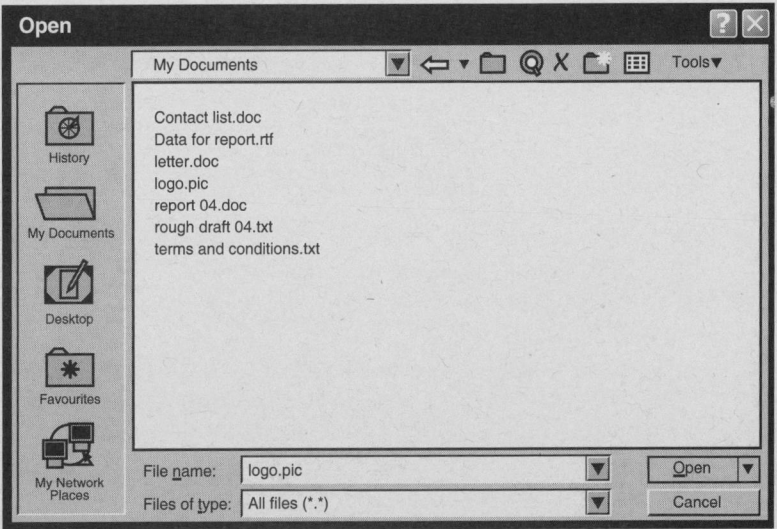

(a) When Alistair tries to insert the file *logo.pic* an error message is displayed.

    (i) Suggest a possible reason why Alistair cannot insert this file.   **1**

    (ii) Explain what he could do to solve his problem.   **1**

(b) Alistair is shown by his friend how to include pictures into word processed documents using *object linking*.

    (i) Explain what is meant by the term object linking.   **1**

    (ii) State **one** advantage and **one** disadvantage of using object linking in a word processed document.   **2**

    (iii) State **one** item of link information that will be stored for the picture.   **1**

(c) Alistair notices that on some occasions when using the software, certain menu items are greyed out at certain times and cannot be selected. Use an example to explain why a menu item may be greyed out.   **2**

(d) Alistair's friend, Campbell, has an older version of the same word processing software. He asks Alistair for a copy of the new version to try out before he buys it himself. Describe **one** social and **one** legal implication of this.   **2**

                                    (10)

[Turn over

Marks

Part A—Computer Application Software (continued)

7. Cozy Carpets has stores throughout Scotland. The home page of the website is shown below and contains a graphic labelled A and a section of text labelled B.

   The company have used a web authoring package and a graphics package to create the website.

(a) The graphic, labelled A, was created in a graphics package and imported into the web authoring package. In order to help minimise the download time, the size of the graphic file will need to be reduced. One method of reducing the size of the graphic file is to resize the graphic; resizing can be done either in the web authoring package or in the graphics package.

    (i) Explain why resizing the graphic in the web authoring package will not reduce the size of the graphic file.   1

    (ii) Describe **two** other methods of reducing the size of the graphic file using the graphics package.   2

(b) Before the home page is published a built-in spellchecker is used. Explain why the spellchecker can be used to check the spelling in the section labelled B but not in the section labelled A in the diagram above.   2

(c) The web authoring package used to create the website is *shareware* whereas the graphics package used is the *full commercial version*. Describe **two** differences between the legal use of each of these versions.   2

(d) Cozy Carpets, along with many other companies, offers the facility for customers to purchase goods on-line. Describe **one** possible consequence of this use of information technology for:

    (i) customers;

    (ii) the company;

    (iii) society.   3

    (10)

    (30)

[END OF SECTION II—PART A]

Part B—Expert Systems

Attempt ALL questions in this part.

Marks

8. Walker & Carnan are financial advisors, who invest money on behalf of clients. They use an expert system to help them produce investment plans.

   (*a*) Give **two** reasons why investment planning is a suitable subject on which to develop an expert system.

   2

   (*b*) Miss Leith invests £10,000 in a 5-year investment plan recommended by the expert system used by Walker & Carnan. After 5 years, her investment is worth only £4,000. Suggest **three** people who could be held responsible for the poor performance of the investment, giving reasons for your answers.

   3

   (*c*) The expert system makes use of *certainty factors*.

      (i) What is a certainty factor?

      1

      (ii) Describe **two** uses of certainty factors within this expert system.

      2

   (*d*) Walker & Carnan advertise their services on the World Wide Web. Their website includes quotes from investors who have increased their initial investment significantly as shown below.

   # Walker and Carnan
   ### FINANCIAL ADVISORS

   Home I News I Pensions I Investments I Insurance I Banks I Shares I Funds I Bonds

   "I invested £100,000 and doubled my money in 3 years"

   Debbie Granger, Anderson Street, Glasgow

   Comment on the social and ethical implications of this use of information technology.

   2

   (10)

[Turn over

Marks

Part B—Expert Systems (continued)

9. Askal has a collection of emeronds. An emerond is a precious stone found on the ocean floor. Emeronds are graded as first, second or third class. Askal has decided to create an expert system to help her grade her emeronds. She consults Professor Rutherford and Professor Slessor who are experts on emeronds.

   Professor Rutherford says:

   Emeronds in prime condition with a round shape are graded first class. An emerond in standard condition is graded second class if it has a square shape, but third class if it has a round shape.

   Professor Slessor says:

   If an emerond is red and rough it is in standard condition, and all yellow emeronds are in standard condition unless they have a glassy texture, in which case they are in prime condition.

   One of the rules in Askal's expert system is shown below:

   IF condition is prime
   AND shape is round
   THEN grading is first class.

   (a) Write the rules required to represent the remainder of the expert knowledge given above. The rules should be expressed in the same form as shown above.   4

   (b) System validation is one of the stages in the production of the expert system. Name and describe **two** other stages.   2

   (c) Three of the emeronds in Askal's collection are described in the table below. What grade, if any, would be given to these by the human experts?

	Colour	Texture	Shape
(i)	Red	Rough	Square
(ii)	Yellow	Glassy	Round
(iii)	Red	Glassy	Square

        3

   (d) Describe how the results from (c) could be used to validate the expert system.   1

   (10)

Part B—Expert Systems (continued)

Marks

10. Cozy Carpets has recently introduced an expert system to assist customers in selecting the most suitable floor coverings. This is available on its website and a sequence of screenshots from the system is shown below.

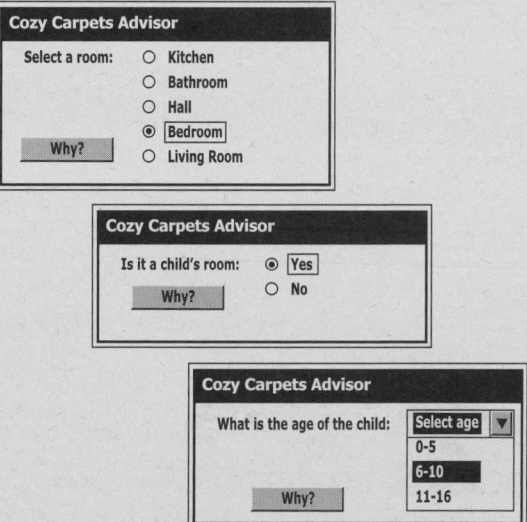

(a) Describe the role of each component of an expert system in producing the sequence of questions shown above.

3

(b) What type of chaining is this system more likely to employ? Justify your answer.

2

(c) The result of a user's consultation with the expert system is shown below.

We recommend that you consider the following.

Floor covering	Manufacturer	Price per sq m	Approximate cost
Laminate	Gala Floors	£5·50	£49·50
Laminate	Strathmore	£12·75	£114·75
Carpet	Hilton	£7·80	£70·20
Carpet	Axminster	£27·50	£247·50

The table of results is selected by the expert system from a database. Compare a database management system (DBMS) and an expert system in terms of:

(i) how data is represented;

(ii) how results are identified.

2

(d) (i) What is the purpose of the "Why" button in the screenshots shown above?

1

(ii) Describe **one** use of this feature for:

• the user;

• the developer of the system.

2

(10)

(30)

[END OF SECTION II—PART B]

Part C—Hypermedia

Attempt ALL questions in this part.

Marks

11. The Scottish Regiments Museum will be opening soon in Edinburgh. Visitors will be able to learn about such regiments as the Gordon Highlanders, the Black Watch and the King's Own Scottish Borderers. The museum plans to include a variety of multimedia and hypermedia presentations.

(*a*) Explain the difference between *multimedia* and *hypermedia*.   **2**

(*b*) Describe **three** elements which could be included in a hypermedia presentation to enhance the experience of visitors to the museum.   **3**

(*c*) It has been decided to develop a touch screen interface for one of the presentations as shown below.

(i) Give **two** reasons why this would be the most suitable interface.   **2**

(ii) With reference to the welcome screen above, describe the structure of the information in terms of nodes, links and anchors.   **3**

    (10)

Marks

Part C—Hypermedia (continued)

12. Two reference models used to describe the architecture of a hypermedia system are the *Dexter model* and the *Amsterdam model*.

    (a) The Dexter model comprises three *layers* linked by two *interfaces*.

        (i) Which **two** layers are linked by anchoring?

        (ii) Which **two** layers are linked by the presentations specification interface?

2

    (b) Describe **three** features found in the Amsterdam model but not in the Dexter model.

3

    (c) The hypermedia system illustrated below is based on the Amsterdam model.

        (i) State the type of component labelled **A**.

1

        (ii) State the type of component labelled **B**.

1

        (iii) Identify the item labelled **C**.

1

    (d) Multimedia components can be *synchronised* in the Amsterdam model.

        State **two** types of synchronisation that could be used and describe the difference between them.

2

(10)

Marks

Part C—Hypermedia (continued)

13. Every year SoundWave radio station organises a UK-wide charity auction held over one weekend. Companies are asked to donate items which are then auctioned to members of the public. This year a website has been created which will allow the public to place their bids on-line. The companies have to e-mail the radio station with details of their donated items before the auction starts. Staff at the radio station then place the item into an appropriate category. Bids for any of the items can be tracked throughout the weekend until the auction closes on the Sunday night.

The homepage of the website is displayed below.

Kirsten was listening to the radio and heard that a 14 ft trampoline had been donated.

(a) She decides to make a bid for this item but has difficulty in locating it by a search or navigation.

Give **one** reason why she may have experienced difficulty using:

  (i) the search facility;   1

  (ii) the navigation facility.   1

Marks

Part C—Hypermedia (continued)

13. (continued)

(*b*) In order to participate in the auction, Kirsten must first complete a website registration form to obtain a username and password. Once she has registered she can make a bid for the trampoline. The registration form and the bid form are shown below.

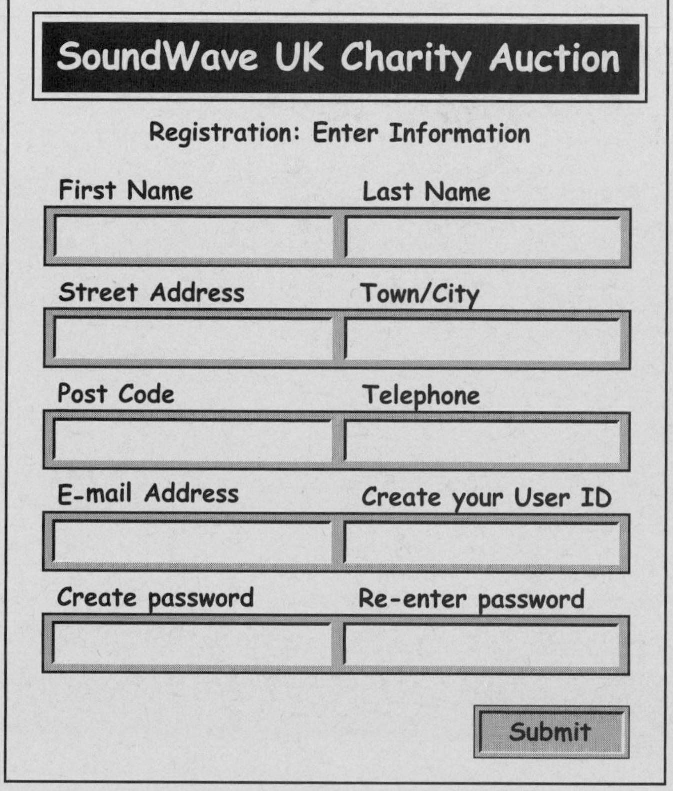

Registration Form

SoundWave UK Charity Auction

Registration: Enter Information

First Name   Last Name

Street Address   Town/City

Post Code   Telephone

E-mail Address   Create your User ID

Create password   Re-enter password

Submit

Bid Form

Make a Bid

Item No.	6564643
Item description	14ft Trampoline
Username	KirstenB
Password	*************
Bid Amount	£120.00

Submit

Explain how a relational database with a web interface is used to operate this auction efficiently.

3

[Turn over for Questions 13(*c*) and 13(*d*) on *Page twenty-two*

Marks

Part C—Hypermedia (continued)

13. (continued)

(c) Kirsten places a bid for the trampoline. The website then displays the following information about the status of the bid.

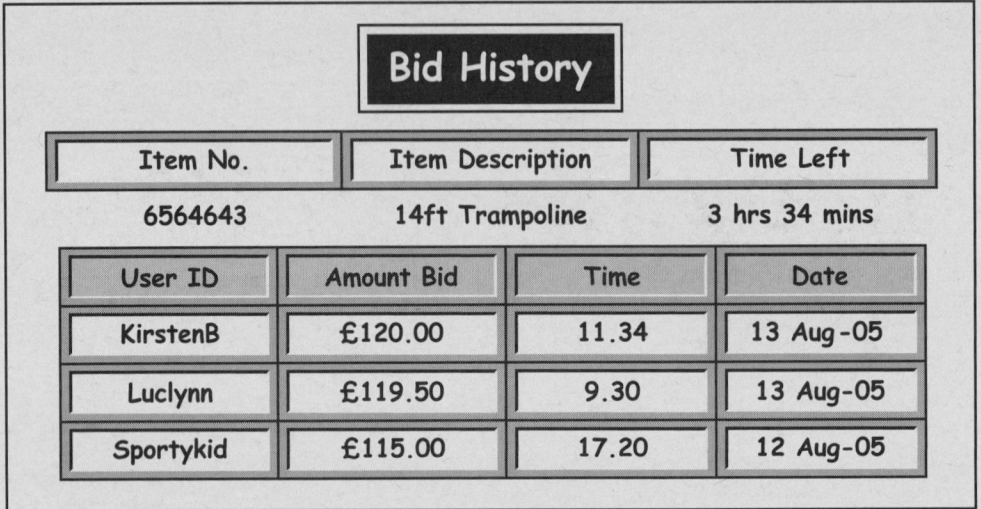

(i) What must Kirsten do to ensure that the latest bids for the trampoline are displayed on her screen?

1

(ii) Kirsten's bid was successful. She would like to pay for the item by credit card. Describe **one** development of website security which allows Kirsten to do this safely.

2

(d) Describe **two** social factors that have contributed to the increased popularity of auction websites like this one.

2

(10)

(30)

[END OF SECTION II—PART C]

[END OF QUESTION PAPER]

[BLANK PAGE]

X216/301

NATIONAL QUALIFICATIONS 2006	THURSDAY, 1 JUNE 9.00 AM – 11.30AM	INFORMATION SYSTEMS HIGHER

Attempt **all** of Section I, **all** of Section II and **one** part of Section III.

Sections I and II — Attempt **all** questions.

Section III — This section has three parts

   Part A—Applied Multimedia

   Part B—Expert Systems

   Part C—The Internet

Choose **one** part and attempt all of the questions in this part.

Read all questions carefully.

Write your answers in the answer book provided. Do not write on the question paper.

Write as neatly as possible.

SCOTTISH QUALIFICATIONS AUTHORITY

SECTION I

Attempt ALL questions in this section.

Marks

1. Kwik Kut employs a number of stylists each of whom has a number of regular customers. Details of appointments are kept in a database created from data in un-normalised form. The sample below shows an entry in the database.

Stylist	Sharon
Appointment Date	23/06/06
Appointment Time	10.00
Customer Name	Pamela Forsyth
Customer Phone Number	01554 775643

   Describe **two** problems that would be encountered when modifying the customer's telephone number in the database.   2

2. Each tutor group in a secondary school is identified by a code made up from its year and tutor's initials. For example, Alice Smith's S3 tutor group has the code S3AS.

   Identify **two** problems associated with using this *meaningful identifier* as a primary key.   2

3. A characteristic of normalised data is that it provides *entity integrity*. State the **two** main features of entity integrity.   2

4. Tayview College stores a copy of each pupil's timetable in the college office. It includes the following data items: Pupil number, Pupil name, Class, Subject.

   Identify a *single-valued attribute* from this structure and give a reason for your choice.   2

5. (*a*) State why an *integer* data type is appropriate for storing the height of a mountain in metres.   1

   (*b*) State the most appropriate data type for storing a person's height in metres.   1

6. What is the purpose of a *data dictionary*?   2

7. State the *cardinality* of each of the following relationships.

   (*a*) Vehicle and Vehicle Registration Number   1

   (*b*) Pupil and SQA Candidate Number   1

Marks

SECTION I (continued)

8. Explain the difference between *data* and *information*. Use an example to illustrate your answer.

   3

9. What is a *distributed database*?

   2

10. The pie chart below shows the votes cast for contestants in a TV reality show. The contestant with the highest number of votes wins.

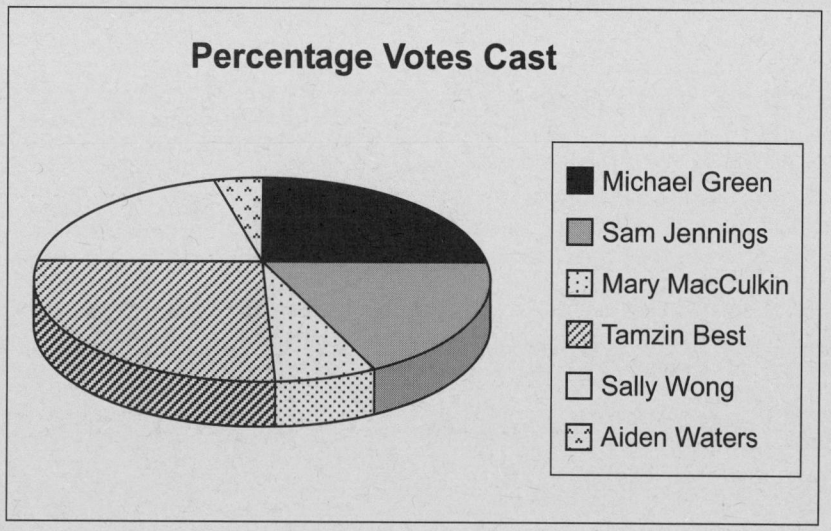

   (a) State the *form* and *type* of the information displayed in the pie chart.

   2

   (b) Comment on the quality of this information in terms of its *level of detail*.

   2

11. What is the purpose of a *management information system*?

   2

12. Identify **one** factor that would have to be considered in a decision to upgrade a company's computer software and state **why** it would be considered.

   2

13. (a) To which **one** of the following countries can personal data **not** be exported under the terms of the Data Protection Act 1998?

   (i) Ireland

   (ii) France

   (iii) United States of America

   (iv) Germany

   1

   (b) Explain your answer to (a).

   2

   (30)

[END OF SECTION I]

[Turn over

Marks

SECTION II

Attempt ALL questions in this section.

14. Invergordon Electrical is a small company supplying electrical goods to a few shops in the local area. Customer orders are recorded on a customer order card as follows.

Customer no: 1324
Customer name: John Andrews
Address: 27 High Street, Abervalley
Telephone: 0123 456 7890 Date: 29/05/06

Item number	Number ordered
555666	14
556789	5
144690	8

Customer no: 1411
Customer name: Electric City
Address: Dunton Lane, Inverdon
Telephone: 01321 222333 Date: 30/05/06

Item number	Number ordered
554321	4
176888	15
555666	9

Details of all items offered for sale are stored on stock cards. Each item is obtained from a single supplier. Part of a stock card is shown below.

Stock Card					
Item number	Description	Supplier name	Supplier address	Supplier telephone	Price
554321	Fineline Portable DVD Player	Acme Artifacts	Industrial Zone, Byway	01998 232 234	£124·99
555666	Megatone MP3 Player 128MB	Consolidated Inc	Manufacture Street, Grayton	01232 657 244	£62·99
144690	Fineline DVD Player	Acme Artifacts	Industrial Zone, Byway	01998 232 234	£26·49
176888	Bigsound Stereo Headphones	Weimakem	Well Road, Blackferry	01987 654 321	£11·75

(a) The present system can be represented in un-normalised form as:

Customer no
Customer name
Customer address
Customer telephone
Order date
Item number
Number ordered
Description
Supplier name
Supplier address
Supplier telephone
Price

(i) Using Customer no as the primary key, "transform" this un-normalised data to first normal form by removing repeating groups. 3

(ii) Identify all primary and foreign keys. 3

Marks

SECTION II (continued)

14. **(continued)**

(*b*) (i) Transform this first normal form to second normal form by removing partial dependencies. 4

(ii) Identify all primary and foreign keys. 2

(*c*) (i) Transform this second normal form to third normal form by removing non-key dependencies. 3

(ii) Identify all primary and foreign keys. 2

15. Douglas Car Rental uses a relational database. The data is held in the following tables.

Car	**Customer**	**Rental**	**Charge**
Car registration	Customer number	Customer number*	Category
Make	Customer name	Car registration*	Price per day
Model	Customer address	Date rented	
Category*		Number of days rented	

(*a*) Draw an entity relationship diagram to represent this data model. 6

(*b*) Each month a report is produced to show the rental income from each car. The report for car registration WZ51 ABC is shown below.

Date	Days	Income
1/10/05	4	£79·96
6/10/05	7	£139·93
15/10/05	2	£39·98
17/10/05	3	£59·97
29/10/05	1	£19·99
Total		£339·83

(i) Name the tables and fields which would be used to produce this report. 5

(ii) State **two** features of the RDBMS which would be used to calculate the monthly total from the income. 2

[Turn over

Marks

SECTION II (continued)

16. Akron Enterprises uses a network file server to hold all the applications regularly used by each department along with all the work of each employee stored in home directories.

    (a) Recommend a back-up strategy for this system.   5

    (b) Head Office has decided to replace the existing word processing package in all its branches with a new one from a different software company. Before reaching its decision the Head Office carries out an evaluation of the software. Two criteria used in this evaluation were availability of training and provision of support.

        (i) State **four** other criteria that could be used to evaluate software.   4

        (ii) Name **two** different methods of providing training.   2

        (iii) Head Office can supply user support in a variety of ways. Identify the most suitable way and justify your answer.   2

    (c) Head Office recommends that all word processed documents conform to a *house style*.

        (i) State **four** features of a house style.   4

        (ii) Describe the easiest way of enabling all users to make use of the house style.   2

Marks

SECTION II (continued)

17. Dundonald Building Ltd is a local construction company which has won the contract to build a new sports centre. The project manager has produced the chart shown below for the building of the sports centre.

Sports Centre Construction								
TASKS	Start Date	End Date	March	April	May	June	July	Cost
Contract Writing	03/03	30/03	▓▓▓					£50,000
Obtain Permits	25/03	04/04	▪					£1,200
Site Work	04/04	30/06		▓▓▓▓▓▓				£1,500,000
Plumbing	28/05	20/06			▓▓▓			£55,000
Electricity	28/05	20/06			▓▓▓			£40,000
Roof	20/06	20/07					▓▓	£22,300
Inspection	22/07	22/07						£1,000

(a) (i) Would this chart be categorised as strategic, tactical or operational information?   1

    (ii) Name this type of chart.   1

    (iii) State the type of software used to produce this chart.   1

    (iv) Other than producing charts, state **two** further uses of this type of software.   2

(b) The project manager has a personal digital assistant (PDA). This has personal information management software installed.

Identify **three** features of this type of software and describe how the project manager would make use of each of these features.   6

(60)

[END OF SECTION II]

[Turn over

SECTION III

Section III—This section has three parts

Choose **one** part and attempt **all** of the questions in this part.

SECTION III

Part A—Applied Multimedia

Marks

Attempt ALL questions in this part.

18. "McDVD Movies" is a business selling DVD movies. It is creating a website to advertise and sell its products.

   (*a*) The website designers are concerned that some customers might get "lost in hyperspace". Name and describe **two** solutions to this problem that could be built into the design of the website.   4

   (*b*) The team producing the website will provide appropriate user documentation. State **three** different areas that should be covered in this documentation.   3

   (*c*) Customers will be able to view clips and trailers of movies which can be streamed or downloaded. Describe **one** advantage of streaming.   2

   (*d*) The company considered producing a DVD to advertise its movies. Give **one** advantage and **one** disadvantage of this method of delivering multimedia development compared to a website.   2

19. The management of West Coast Coasters decided to produce a multimedia virtual tour of the company's theme park. They discussed this project brief with Multi-Scot-Media, a multimedia development company. A contractual requirements specification was then drawn up.

   (*a*) The project manager from Multi-Scot-Media took part in the discussions with West Coast Coasters. Give **two** examples of details that the project manager would need clarified by West Coast Coasters in order to draw up the contractual requirements specification.   2

   (*b*) The multimedia designer from Multi-Scot-Media created a detailed storyboard for the project.

   (i) Describe **two** multimedia elements that could be used to enhance a virtual reality tour of a theme park.   4

   (ii) Give **one** piece of information about one of these elements that would be included in the detailed storyboard.   1

   (*c*) The designer has made use of metaphors in the virtual reality tour. Describe a metaphor that would be suitable for use in this virtual tour.   3

[Turn over

Marks

SECTION III

Part A—Applied Multimedia (continued)

20. A group of sixth year pupils has to produce a multimedia presentation about their business project to be shown to the whole year group.

    (*a*) State a suitable type of navigation structure for the presentation and give a reason for your answer.   3

    (*b*) Each member of the team is responsible for the design of one slide in the presentation. Explain why this approach may affect the quality of the design of the presentation.   2

    (*c*) The diagram below shows the title slide as produced by one of the pupils. Describe how the display of media elements in this slide could be improved by the use of:

        (i) kerning;   2

        (ii) anti-aliasing.   2

Marks

SECTION III

Part A—Applied Multimedia (continued)

21. A shopping centre provides a kiosk for customers to access multimedia information about some of its stores. A jewellery store decides to advertise its services by including an interactive multimedia display in the kiosk. This display can be updated monthly.

    (*a*) Suggest a suitable interface for the multimedia information in the kiosk and give a reason for your answer. **2**

    (*b*) Comment on the quality of information provided by the kiosk in terms of completeness and availablity. **4**

    (*c*) Explain why the store may need to produce the media elements itself rather than use suitable files already available on the World Wide Web. **2**

22. A car manufacturer provides access in its dealers' showrooms to online photographs of each model.

    (*a*) The graphics were saved in JPEG format. Give **two** reasons for choosing JPEG rather than TIFF or GIF in this situation. **4**

    (*b*) The colour in the photograph does not appear the same when displayed on different computers. Why is this and what can be done to solve this problem? **3**

    (*c*) The manufacturer's handbook advises customers to get help with some enquiries at

    http://www.eurcar.com/customers/support/faq.htm

    (i) Identify and name **three** parts of the structure of this URL. **3**

    (ii) State whether this is an absolute or relative URL and justify your choice. **2**

    (50)

[END OF SECTION III—PART A]

Marks

SECTION III

Part B—Expert Systems

Attempt ALL questions in this part.

23. Companies involved in extracting mineral deposits such as oil and iron ore make use of a range of computer-based information systems, including decision support systems and expert systems.

    (a) Distinguish between a *decision support system* and an *expert system*. **4**

    (b) The PROSPECTOR expert system was developed for use by mining companies. Describe this expert system in terms of its *category*, *domain*, and main *characteristics*. **4**

24. Drumuille College has over 5000 students attending classes in 102 courses in 64 classrooms, lecture theatres and practical rooms. Every year, it takes a member of staff several weeks to plan the timetable to ensure all the classes can take place as required.

    (a) Give **two** reasons why this timetabling problem may be a suitable subject on which to develop an expert system. **2**

    (b) Describe **two** factors which the college should consider before deciding whether to develop the expert system. **2**

    (c) The following predicates represent statements about student and classes.

Predicate	Statement
takes(alison, catering2)	Alison takes the Catering2 course
class(2031, 45, catering2)	Class 2031 has 45 students in the Catering2 course
in_class(alison, 2031)	Alison is in class 2031

    Represent the following statements using predicate logic.

    (i) Fiona takes the *Tourism* course and the *Leisure Management* course. **2**

    (ii) All students who take *Catering1* also take *Food Hygiene* in class 1023. **6**

    (d) Distinguish between an expert system and a relational database in terms of how data is represented and the method of querying. **4**

    (e) Explain what is meant by a deductive database. **2**

Marks

SECTION III

Part B—Expert Systems (continued)

25. Crossandra is a type of house plant from the East Indies with green pointed leaves and spikes of bright orange flowers. Unfortunately, it is not the easiest type of house plant to look after, and a degree of expertise is required to keep a plant from one year to the next.

Information about what can go wrong is shown in the following expert system rules.

IF   rot on leaves
THEN   the conditions are too wet and humid (0·6).

IF   the leaves are limp
THEN   the plant has been over watered (0·8).

IF   the leaves drop AND
          there is no plant growth
THEN   the plant is too cold (0·8).

IF   the leaves shrivel
THEN   the plant is too hot and dry (0·9).

IF   the plant wilts AND
          the leaves drop
THEN   the conditions are too draughty (0·7).

Suppose the following facts about a crossandra plant are observed with the certainty factors given.

The leaves are limp	0·5
The plant wilts	0·7
The leaves drop	0·9
There is no growth	0·6

(a) Calculate the certainty of the conclusion that the plant is too cold. Show your working.   **2**

(b) Which conclusion will be drawn from the given facts? Explain your answer.   **3**

(c) This expert system uses a forward chaining inferencing strategy. In a forward chaining system, explain:

  (i) why *conflict resolution* is necessary;   **2**

  (ii) the purpose of the RETE algorithm;   **2**

  (iii) how the *specificity* conflict resolution strategy works.   **2**

[Turn over

Marks

SECTION III

Part B—Expert Systems (continued)

26. The following paragraph outlines a limited domain of knowledge about growing azaleas in various types of garden soil. This knowledge is to be represented by an expert system using an expert system shell. A user of the expert system should be given advice about the likely success of growing an azalea in their garden given the colour of the soil.

A	Garden soils are generally one of three types: acid, loam or clay. Acid soils are dark in colour, loams are brown and clay soils are light in colour.
B	Acid soils are most suitable for growing coniferous trees, rhododendrons and azaleas.
C	Loam soils are usually suitable for most types of garden plants.
D	Clay soils are often lumpy and difficult to drain. They are light in colour. Few plants will grow well in clay soils.

Name an expert system shell with which you are familiar.

(a) Represent the knowledge contained in paragraph A above, to conclude a soil's type, given its colour.

3

(b) In paragraphs B – D, identify **two** words which indicate uncertainty in the information.

2

(c) Represent the knowledge in paragraphs B and C, to give the conclusion "The soil is suitable for growing azaleas". Your rules should refer to your answer to (a), and include an appropriate certainty factor.

4

Marks

SECTION III

Part B—Expert Systems (continued)

27. Consider a forward chaining expert system containing the following rule base, where letters P – W represent facts which are known or can be concluded.

1   If P and V then X.

2   If P and S then V.

3   If P and Q then V.

4   If P and R then T.

5   If P and R and T then W.

6   If P and Q and R then U.

Suppose the working memory contains the facts P, Q and R, added in that order.

(*a*)   Which rules exist in the conflict set?   **2**

(*b*)   (i)   Which rule will fire using a *first-come-first-served* (also known as *rule ordering*) conflict resolution strategy?   **1**

         (ii) Which rule will fire using the "specificity" conflict resolution strategy?   **1**

                                                                                                 (50)

[END OF SECTION III—PART B]

SECTION III

Part C—The Internet

Attempt ALL questions in this part.

Marks

28. The diagram below represents part of the network at Interworld Travel Agency.

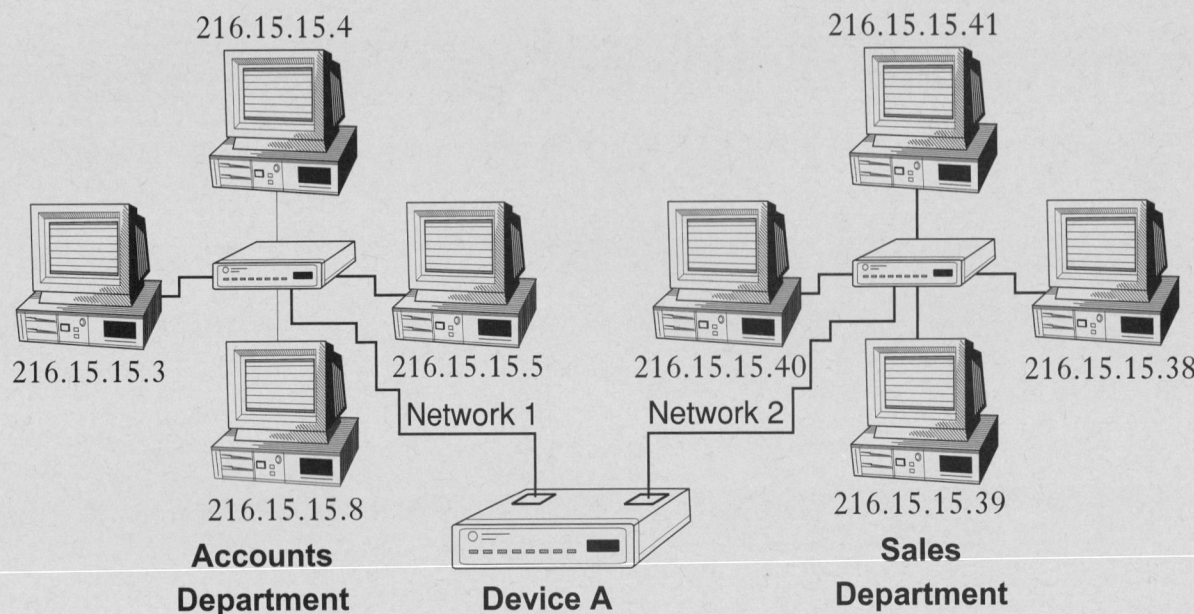

216.15.15.4
216.15.15.41
216.15.15.3
216.15.15.5
Network 1
216.15.15.40
Network 2
216.15.15.38
216.15.15.8
216.15.15.39
Accounts
Department
Device A
Sales
Department

Priya has just started work in the sales department and has been given a new computer. A member of the IT department arrived to set up her computer and entered the following information.

IP Address: 216.15.15.45

Subnet Mask: 255.255.255.224

Gateway: 216.15.15.34

(a) To what class does the IP address **216.15.15.45** belong? 1

(b) The accounts department and the sales department are on different subnets.

   (i) Using the above subnet mask, how many subnets can Interworld have? 2

   (ii) What is the maximum number of hosts on any of the subnets? 2

(c) Device A has two IP addresses, 216.15.15.2 and 216.15.15.34.

   (i) What type of device is device A? 1

   (ii) Why does device A have two IP addresses? 2

SECTION III

Marks

Part C—The Internet (continued)

28. (continued)

(d)   On another screen, the IT engineer enters

Proxy Server :server1.iwta.co.uk

(i)   What is a proxy server?

2

(ii)   Give **two** reasons why Interworld would use a proxy server.

2

(e)   The engineer returns to his computer and adds Priya's username and password to the proxy server using Telnet. What is Telnet?

2

29.   Describe the role of each of the following Internet regulatory organisations.

(a)   Internet Assigned Numbers Authority (IANA)

1

(b)   The World Wide Web Consortium (W3C)

1

30.   The screenshot below shows the home page of a website which has CDs and DVDs available for download.

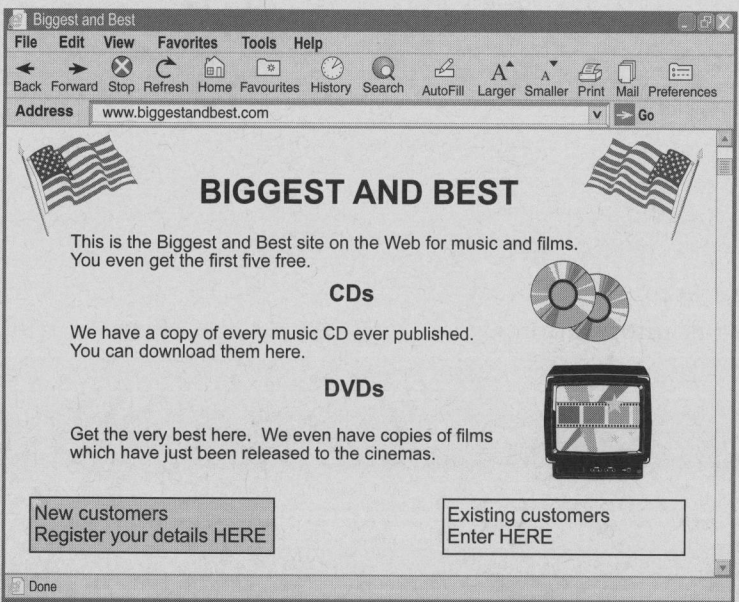

(a)   Which protocol translates a URL into an IP address?

1

(b)   Assess this web resource with reference to credibility and legality.

4

(c)   The web page was created using a web authoring package. Give **one** advantage and **one** disadvantage of using this method compared to writing HTML code.

2

(d)   Biggest and Best could make use of cookies to enhance a user's experience of their website.

(i)   What is a cookie?

2

(ii)   Describe **two** ways in which Biggest and Best could make use of cookies.

4

SECTION III

Marks

Part C—The Internet (continued)

31. Sean and Lorraine are university lecturers who are collaborating in making up the final year examination. Lorraine had recently taken a visiting lecturer post overseas but is continuing to work on the examination paper. She and Sean exchange possible examination questions using PGP to ensure the security of the material.

    (a) What method does PGP use to encrypt and decrypt messages?

    2

    (b) Describe how Lorraine would use PGP to send a message to Sean.

    4

32. Strathmore IT Solutions has been asked by a client to develop a website showing pictures of its products. A developer has produced the following template.

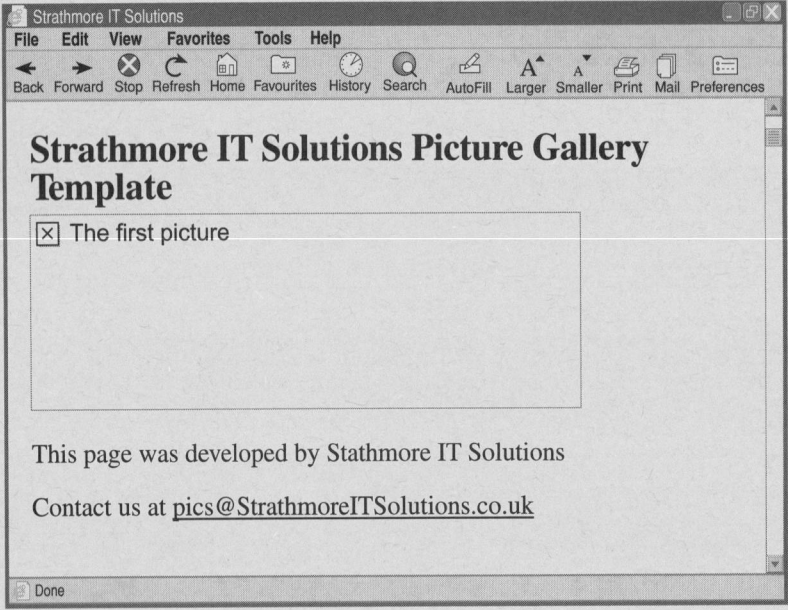

Part of the HTML code used to produce this template is as follows.

```
1    <HTML>
2    <HEAD>
3    <TITLE>Strathmore IT Solutions</TITLE>
4    </HEAD>
5    <BODY>
6    <P>
7    <H2> Strathmore IT Solutions Picture Gallery Template </H2>
8    <IMG SRC="../images/picture1.jpg" WIDTH=525 HEIGHT=104 ALT
     ="The first picture" BORDER=0>
9    <BR>
10   <P>
11   This page was developed by Strathmore IT Solutions
12   <P>
13
14   <P>
15   </BODY>
16   </HTML>
```

Page eighteen

SECTION III

Part C—The Internet (continued)

32. **(continued)**

(a) The text "Strathmore IT Solutions Picture Gallery Template" is too large. Rewrite the line of code which would display this in a slightly smaller size.

2

(b) The WIDTH and HEIGHT attributes of the IMG tag, as in row 8, define the displayed size of a graphic. How does including these attributes benefit the user?

3

(c) In what way does the <BR> tag differ from the <P> tag?

2

(d) Line 13 should contain the HTML code to allow users to click on the underlined text pics@StrathmoreITSolutions.co.uk to send a message to the company. Write the line of code required to display the line in the template which begins

"Contact us at pics@StrathmoreITSolutions.co.uk"

and will allow the users to send their message by clicking on the underlined text.

4

(e) Uniformity of presentation is one characteristic of site design. Name **two** further characteristics of site design and evaluate the above site in terms of these characteristics.

4

(50)

[END OF SECTION III—PART C]

[END OF QUESTION PAPER]

[BLANK PAGE]

[BLANK PAGE]

X216/301

NATIONAL QUALIFICATIONS 2007	THURSDAY, 24 MAY 9.00 AM – 11.30AM	INFORMATION SYSTEMS HIGHER

Attempt **all** of Section I, **all** of Section II and **one** part of Section III.

Sections I and II — Attempt **all** questions.

Section III — This section has three parts, choose **one** part and attempt all of the questions in this part.

      Part A—Applied Multimedia

      Part B—Expert Systems

      Part C—The Internet

Read all questions carefully.

Write your answers in the answer book provided. Do not write on the question paper.

Write as neatly as possible.

SCOTTISH
QUALIFICATIONS
AUTHORITY
©

SECTION I

Attempt ALL questions in this section.

Marks

1. Below is a sample taken from a travel agency's holiday booking database. All data is held in a single table.

Booking reference	HT6745
Date of arrival	21/07/07
Length of stay	7 nights
Hotel name	Hilton
Hotel location	Glasgow
Customer name	John Jackson
Customer address	25 Brighton Place, Hamilton
Customer telephone number	02654 576431

   Describe **one** problem with deleting a holiday booking record from this database.   2

2. A driving licence number is a *meaningful identifier* made up from data based on a person's surname, date of birth and initials. For example,

   SMITH 804017 AA3QZ

   The last 3 characters are generated randomly.

   (a) Explain why the last 3 characters must be included for the driving licence number to be used as a primary key.   2

   (b) Describe a problem in using the driving licence number as a primary key.   2

3. What is a *foreign key* in a relational database?   2

4. A characteristic of normalised data is that it allows for *referential integrity*. Define the term *referential integrity*.   2

5. KwikShop supermarket stores information about each customer sales transaction. It uses the structure

   TRANSACTION(Transaction Number, Till Number, Operator, Item, Price)

   (a) Identify a *multi-valued attribute* from this structure and give a reason for your choice.   2

   (b) State what is meant by the *domain* of an attribute.   2

   (c) State **one** *domain constraint* which might apply to the Operator attribute.   1

6. Define the term *knowledge*.   2

7. Describe **one** use hospitals make of *expert systems*.   2

Marks

SECTION I (continued)

8. The chart below shows results of a survey of customer satisfaction with the standard of food at a motorway service area.

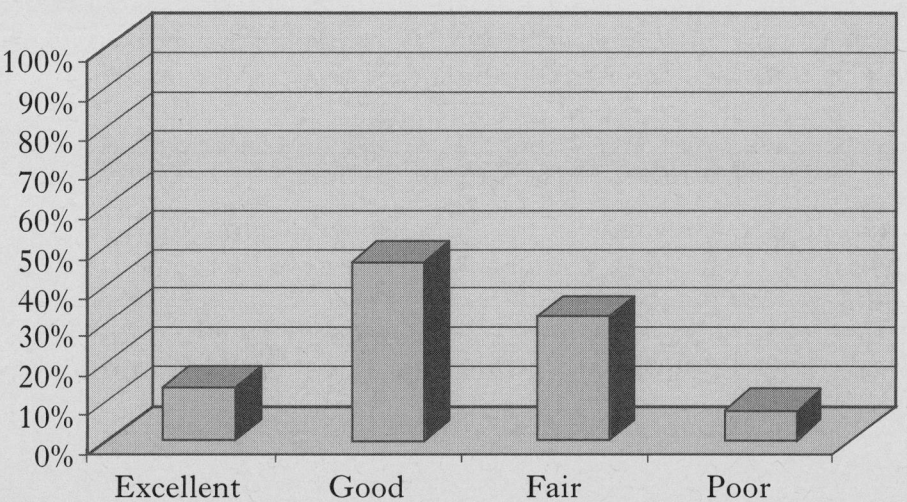

(a) Explain how this information can be both *quantitative* and *qualitative*.   2

(b) State **one** factor which may affect the reliability of the information.   1

9. An *executive information system* (EIS) is used at the strategic level of an organisation. Describe **one** function of an EIS that supports decision making at this level.   2

10. Other than cost, state **two** criteria for evaluating computer software.   2

11. Describe **two** steps which employers should take to comply with Health and Safety regulations for those working with computer equipment.   2

12. State the purpose of the Regulation of Investigatory Powers Act (2000).   2

               (30)

[END OF SECTION I]

[Turn over

SECTION II

Marks

Attempt ALL questions in this section.

13. Discovery Gym Club keeps records of club members' fitness and performance levels on record cards. Each member of the gym has a trainer who recommends exercises for the club member. When an exercise is carried out, the equipment used calculates a performance score based on how well the user performed the exercise. The club member writes the date of the exercise and performance scores for each exercise on a record card as shown below.

Member Performance Record

Member name: Andrew Johnstone   **Member no:** 97842
Member address: 27 High Street, Craigbank   **Trainer:** W Lennon
Member telephone: 01235 457632

Date	Exercise ID	Equipment	Duration	Level	Performance Score
26/06/07	EB21	Exercise Bike	10	5	13
26/06/07	ST04	Stepper	15	4	15
28/06/07	EB21	Exercise Bike	10	5	14
28/06/07	ST04	Stepper	15	4	16
28/06/07	ST05	Stepper	15	5	14
28/06/07	EB22	Exercise Bike	12	6	15

Member Performance Record

Member name: Chris Lee   **Member no:** 41845
Member address: 42 Low Road, Craigbank   **Trainer:** C Kent
Member telephone: 01235 439582

Date	Exercise ID	Equipment	Duration	Level	Performance Score
26/06/07	EB21	Exercise Bike	10	5	16
26/06/07	ST04	Stepper	15	4	15
26/06/07	CT17	Cross Trainer	15	3	16
27/06/07	ST04	Stepper	15	4	16
27/06/07	TM27	Treadmill	25	6	17
28/06/07	EB22	Exercise Bike	12	6	12

Only registered trainers are permitted to devise exercise programs for members. Details of trainers are stored as follows:

Discovery Gym Club
Registered Trainers List

Trainer ID	Trainer name	Trainer address	Trainer telephone
01231	W Lennon	42 Wilson Avenue, Doonbrae	01233 665571
01245	C Lamont	11 The Glebe, Strathcraig	01222 699123
01249	L Lamont	11 The Glebe, Strathcraig	01222 699123
01258	C Kent	42 Willow Place, Doonbrae	01233 423145

- Each exercise has a unique Exercise ID and is for a fixed duration and level.
- Trainers insist that the performance score for each exercise is recorded only **once** per day.

Marks

SECTION II (continued)

13. (continued)

(*a*) Data from these records can be represented in un-normalised form as:

Member no
Member name
Member address
Member telephone
Date
Exercise ID
Equipment
Duration
Level
Performance score
Trainer ID
Trainer name
Trainer address
Trainer telephone

    (i) Using <u>Member no</u> as the primary key, transform this un-normalised data to first normal form by removing repeating groups.   **3**

    (ii) Identify all primary and foreign keys.   **3**

(*b*) (i) Transform this first normal form to second normal form by removing partial dependencies.   **4**

    (ii) Identify all primary and foreign keys.   **2**

(*c*) (i) Transform this second normal form to third normal form by removing non-key dependencies.   **3**

    (ii) Identify all primary and foreign keys.   **2**

[Turn over

Marks

SECTION II (continued)

14. Strathcraig Holidays is a firm of travel agents. It has set up a booking system using a relational database. The data is held in the following tables:

Customer	**Holiday**	**Hotel**	**Booking**
Customer ID	Holiday ID	Hotel ID	Customer ID*
Customer name	Duration (nights)	Hotel name	Holiday ID*
Customer address	Date	Hotel address	
Customer phone	Price		
	All inclusive		
	Hotel ID*		

(a) Draw an entity relationship diagram to represent this data model. **6**

(b) The forms shown below are used to enter holiday details into the database.

The data dictionary shown below represents the **Holiday** entity. It has a number of missing entries which are highlighted as A, B, C, D, E, F and G. With reference to the forms shown above, state a suitable entry for each of the **seven** missing values.

Name	Data Type	Validation	Required	Key
Holiday ID	A		Y	PK
Duration (Nights)	B	D	Y	
Date	Date		Y	
Price	Real	E	Y	
All inclusive	C		Y	
Hotel ID	Integer	F	Y	G

7

Marks

SECTION II (continued)

15. Discovery Designs Ltd is a web design company with a network of over 50 computers. Each department of Discovery Designs Ltd is allocated a budget for the financial year. Mr MacGregor, manager of the Accounts Department, decides this year to use his allocation to purchase a new word processing package for his department. Mr MacGregor's decision may cause problems for his department and other users in the company.

(*a*) Describe **four** potential problems that may arise. **8**

(*b*) State **two** types of strategy that the company should put in place to prevent this situation occurring. **2**

[Turn over

SECTION II (continued)

Marks

16. The Mathematics Department of Dee Valley College uses the following spreadsheet to record marks and automatically generate grades and bands.

	A	B	C	D	E
1	Maths Department		Ms H Smyth		2006
2	Prelim Results				
3	Forename	Surname	Mark	Grade	Band
4	Peter	McLean	62	B	4
5	Jonathon	Spence	49	F	Fail
6	Sally	Ferguson	56	C	5
7	Hugh	MacNab	54	C	6
8	Louise	Simpson	58	C	5
9	Nicole	Wyness	43	F	Fail
10	Thomas	Benzie	65	B	3
11	Anthony	Peterson	75	A	2
12	Duncan	Jarvis	61	B	4
13	Ashley	Morrison	88	A	1
14					
15	No of pupils present		10		

The cut-off scores for grades are as follows:

A	70
B	60
C	50

Any mark less than 50 is awarded a grade F.

(a) Write down a suitable formula for cell C15. **2**

(b) Using the IF function, write down a suitable formula for cell D4. **4**

(c) The formula in cell E4 uses the following table to display the appropriate band.

	G	H
1	Mark	Band
2	0	Fail
3	50	6
4	55	5
5	60	4
6	65	3
7	70	2
8	85	1

The formula is made up of several parts. It uses a function with two necessary arguments as shown below.

= _____ A _____ (_____ B _____ , _____ C _____)

(i) Describe the function labelled A.

(ii) Describe the necessary arguments labelled B and C. **4**

Marks

SECTION II (continued)

17. A company uses software to monitor employees' usage of its network.

    (*a*) Why might the company choose to monitor network usage in this way?   **2**

    (*b*) Describe **one** method of monitoring employees' use of the network.   **2**

    (*c*) Comment on the ethics and legality of monitoring employees in this way.   **4**

    (*d*) An employee applies to the company under the Freedom of Information (Scotland) Act (2002) to see the full monitoring reports for the company. Is the employee entitled to this information? Give a reason for your answer.   **2**

    (60)

[END OF SECTION II]

[Turn over

SECTION III

Section III—This section has three parts, choose **one** part and attempt **all** of the questions in this part.

SECTION III

Part A—Applied Multimedia

Marks

Attempt ALL questions in this part.

18. Simon is studying a computing course at college. The course requirements state that students have to complete a project to help the local community. Simon has agreed to help the local primary school develop a multimedia product. The Head Teacher has e-mailed the following project brief to Simon.

> *Dear Simon*
>
> *Could you please develop a stand alone multimedia product to help children learn the basic Road Safety code.*
>
> *Yours sincerely*
>
> *Mrs Adams*
> *Head Teacher*

(a) State **three** further pieces of information Simon would require which have been omitted from the project brief.

3

After the project brief has been clarified, a *requirements specification* is drawn up.

(b) Explain why this document is important.

3

(c) State the most important type of *user interface* for this product. Justify your choice.

3

Simon has created an *outline storyboard* for the product. Children are able to choose traffic conditions, the time of day and a hedgehog to cross the road.

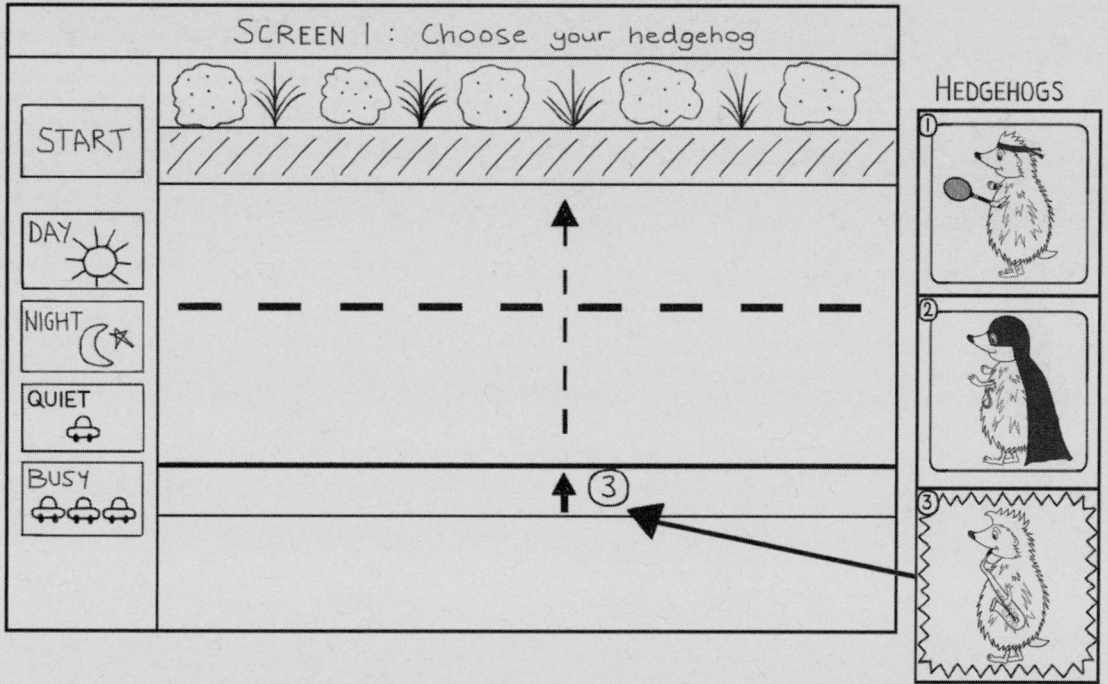

(d) State **three** additional pieces of information that Simon should include in the detailed storyboard.

3

Marks

SECTION III

Part A—Applied Multimedia (continued)

18. (continued)

(*e*) Composite/Hybrid is one type of navigation structure.

State **two** further types of navigation structure and describe how each of these would affect the operation of Simon's product. **6**

(*f*) Simon has decided to create this product using *authoring* software. Justify his choice by describing **two** features of this type of software. **4**

(*g*) In this product, children are allowed to choose a hedgehog and name it.

How is this similar to the way in which many people communicate on the Internet? Give **one** example to illustrate your answer. **4**

19. Testing is an important stage in the development of a multimedia product.

(*a*) State **four** aspects of a product that would be tested during *screen testing*. **4**

(*b*) Describe how *usability testing* is carried out. **2**

20. Virtual Vet would like to develop an interactive computer simulation specifically aimed at providing training and support for Veterinary students. Students would be able to use this product to train on virtual animal bodies.

(*a*) Before the project can begin, the company needs to fill a vacancy that has arisen within the multimedia development team. An advertisement is placed in the local paper for a *multimedia designer*.

The multimedia designer would have to liaise closely with other personnel within the multimedia development team.

State **two** of these personnel and describe their roles in creating this product. **6**

(*b*) Describe **three** examples of how multimedia elements could be used in this product. **6**

Marks

SECTION III

Part A—Applied Multimedia (continued)

21. Strathmobile Telecom is launching a new company logo. Graphic designers have produced a logo in colour. The company intends to use the logo on all its merchandising including posters, magazine advertising, television and website.

    (a) The colour depth of the logo is reduced before it is used on the website. One reason for this is to reduce the file size of the image. State **one** other reason for reducing colour depth.

    2

    (b) Describe **one** problem that may be caused by reducing the colour depth and explain how this problem can be solved.

    4

    (50)

[END OF SECTION III—PART A]

Marks

SECTION III

Part B—Expert Systems

Attempt ALL questions in this part.

22. Dragons of Discovery is a computer game with the object of attacking dragons in order to capture their magical teeth. The user is given advice from a character called Mogo. The advice is generated by an expert system. Here are some of the rules which are used to determine the advice given.

IF dragon IS sleeping
AND dragon can breathe fire
AND dragon IS hungry
THEN Advice IS Attack with magic CF 90.

IF dragon IS sleeping
AND dragon IS hungry
THEN Advice IS Attack with sword CF 80.

IF dragon IS sleeping
AND dragon can breathe fire
THEN Advice IS Attack with lance CF 70.

The following facts are known with the certainty factors given.
Dragon is sleeping 60%
Dragon can breathe fire 80%
Dragon is hungry 40%

(a) (i) Calculate the certainty of the advice "Attack with magic". Show your working. **2**

(ii) What advice would Mogo give based on the rules shown? Explain your answer. **4**

(b) Here are the rules which are used to determine if the dragon is angry.

IF it is raining
THEN the dragon is awake.

IF the dragon is awake
AND the goblins are dancing
THEN the dragon is angry.

Draw a rule tree to show how Mogo could give the reasons for concluding "The dragon is angry". **3**

(c) The expert system uses *forward chaining*. In a forward chaining expert system:

(i) explain what is meant by the *working memory*; **2**

(ii) explain what is meant by a *conflict set*; **2**

(iii) explain how a conflict set is identified; **2**

(iv) describe how the *specificity* conflict resolution strategy works. **2**

SECTION III

Marks

Part B—Expert Systems (continued)

23. The members of a knitting group are graded by their knitting experience, as grade 1, grade 2 or grade 3. A knitting expert system advises members on suitable patterns according to the members' knitting experience. The expert system makes use of the following information.

A	A grade 1 member is one who has never knitted anything before. Members who have knitted a scarf are classed as grade 2. Members are classed as grade 3 if they have knitted a jumper, gloves or socks.
B	The art of knitting involves following a pattern which describes the stitches to be used and colours and types of wool. Simple patterns involve using a single colour of wool and a single type of stitch. Complex patterns involve using a mix of colours of wool or a combination of different stitches or both.
C	Grade 1 members are only able to attempt a simple pattern. Grade 2 members can tackle complex patterns for scarves and simple patterns for socks and jumpers. Grade 3 members can tackle all knitting patterns.

(a) Using a factor table, represent the knowledge contained in paragraph B above. The factor table should show the pattern types and whether there are one or many colours or stitches.

4

(b) The following rule indicates whether a member can knit a complex scarf pattern:

> IF garment IS scarf
> AND pattern IS complex
> AND grading IS > 1
> THEN member can knit garment.

Represent the knowledge contained in paragraph C above to provide advice on the suitability of patterns for knitting scarves, jumpers, gloves and socks, given a member's knitting experience. The rules should be of the form IF <conditions> THEN <conclusions> as shown above.

4

(c) The knitting experience of the group can also be represented as a series of predicates, as follows:

Predicate	Statement
has_knitted(janet, scarf, complex)	Janet has knitted a complex scarf
grade(calum, grade_1)	Calum is graded Grade 1.

Represent the following statements in predicate logic:

(i) Ailsa is Grade 3 and has knitted a complex jumper;

2

(ii) anyone who has knitted simple socks is graded grade 2.

3

SECTION III

Marks

Part B—Expert Systems (continued)

24. Expert systems are used in a wide range of subject domains. Describe the *domain*, *category* and *main characteristics* of the DENDRAL expert system.

4

25. Alison uses a route planning website to help her plan a journey from her home in Dundee to see her aunt and uncle who live in Kington.

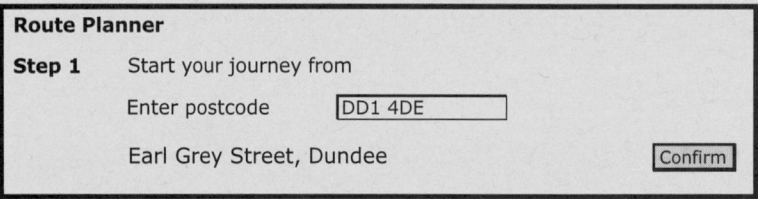

She enters the postcodes of her starting point and destination, and can also specify whether she wants the fastest route, shortest route, or a route that avoids motorways or toll roads and bridges.

(a) When Alison clicks on the Check Details button, the following screen is displayed in which she is asked to confirm the address of the start and end points of her journey, as shown.

```
Route Planner

Step 1    Start your journey from

          Enter postcode      DD1 4DE

          Earl Grey Street, Dundee              Confirm
```

Explain how a database could be used to provide the additional information.

2

(b) The route planner makes use of an expert system to produce the route plan. Describe **two** reasons why route planning is a suitable domain for an expert system.

4

(c) The expert system provides a detailed route which includes a total distance and estimated time.

(i) Alison decides to check an alternative route planning website which also uses an expert system. She finds that the recommended route from this website is longer than the route from the first website.

Describe **three** reasons why the routes may be different.

6

(ii) When Alison makes her journey, she finds that it takes her 1 hour longer than indicated on the route plan.

Describe **two** limitations of a route planning expert system which may have contributed to this result.

4

[END OF SECTION III—PART B]

(50)

Marks

SECTION III

Part C—The Internet

Attempt ALL questions in this part.

26. MP3s4Sale is a web-based company which sells MP3 recordings of local bands via the World Wide Web. The home page at present is shown below.

MP3s4Sale

The following acts and performances have been added this week

- China Cats – Diesel Hi-lites
- East Coast Boys – Who Me?
- Halos – No Angel

+27 more

Click here for list of all new additions   Click here for list of all 1239 files

---

The owners of MP3s4Sale would like to alter the image of the company and have some changes made to the website. The company name is to appear on every page in size h1, colour red, centre aligned and in Arial font.

(a) The company have used Cascading Style Sheets in their website design.

   (i) State what is meant by *Cascading Style Sheets*. **2**

   (ii) Describe how the use of *Cascading Style Sheets* will make it easier to implement this uniformity of presentation. **2**

   (iii) Part of the style sheet the company used is shown below.

```
1.      h1
2.      {text-align : centre
3.
4.
5.      }
```

Write lines 3 and 4 for this style sheet to produce the required effect. **2**

   (iv) The company has produced the correct external style sheet but the heading is displayed in black and left aligned. Describe **two** reasons why this has happened. **4**

   (v) Styles were introduced by The World Wide Web Consortium (W3C). Describe the role of the W3C and describe how it differs from that of the Internet Engineering Task Force (IETF). **4**

(b) The website requires updating every week since new MP3s are added every week. Describe how this site could be implemented by using *dynamic* web pages. **3**

SECTION III

Part C—The Internet (continued)

Marks

27. A group of students are considering starting an on-line business. The home page for their company is shown below.

Academic Solutions

The Final Word in University and College Study Guides

Our Study Guides will cover all courses at any University or College

Pick your subject below.
95 % of our customers pass with merit.

Accounting	Art History	Bioengineering
Biology	Business Administration	Chemistry
Chinese	Civil Engineering	More . . .

E-mail us with any special requirements
Confidentiality Guaranteed – Study Guides sent as encrypted e-mails.

(a) The students apply to Nominet to register gradewhackers.ac.uk as the domain name.

    (i)   Are they likely to be successful?   **1**

    (ii)   Give **two** reasons to justify your answer.   **2**

The URL of the home page would be http://gradewhackers.ac.uk/home.html

(b) Explain how the Domain Name Server (DNS) protocol would allow this home page to be located and displayed in a browser.   **3**

(c) The transfer of the home page from server to client will make use of routers and routing tables.

Define the terms *router* and *routing table* and describe the part played by both in the transfer of data through the Internet.   **8**

(d) Comment on the *credibility* of the information displayed on the homepage.   **4**

(e) The Study Guides are sent as encrypted e-mails. Name and describe a method which can be used for exchanging encrypted e-mail.   **4**

SECTION III

Marks

Part C—The Internet (continued)

28. Below is an extract from Hotel Paradiso's home page showing some of the rooms available. The HTML code used to produce the page is illustrated below the extract.

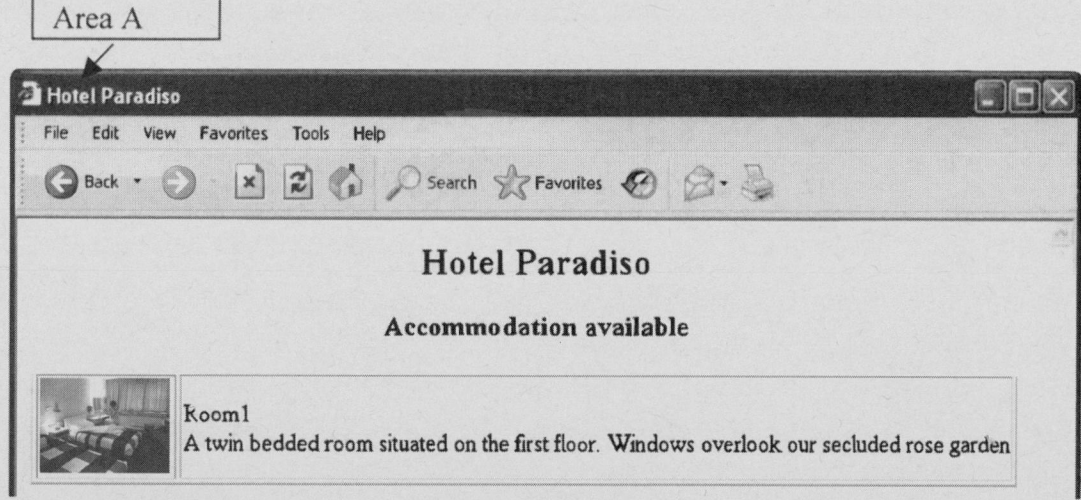

```
1.  <html>
2.  <head>
3.
4.  </head>
5.  <body>
6.  <div align = "centre">
7.  <h2> Hotel Paradiso </h2>
8.  <h3> Accommodation available </h3>
9.  </div>
10. <table>
11.
12. <td> <img src = "Images/Room1thumb.jpg"> </td>
13. <td>Room1.<br> A twin bedded room situated on the first floor.
    Windows overlook our secluded rose garden </td>
14. </tr>
15.
16. </body>
17. </html>
```

(a) Complete the HTML code required in line 3 to display "Hotel Paradiso" in area A.

2

(b) What is the purpose of the <div> tag as used in line 6?

3

(c) The hotel management would like a user to be able to click on the small picture of the room to open a larger picture on a new page. The larger image is stored as "Room1.jpg" in the folder named "Images".

Rewrite the code in line 12 in order to achieve this.

4

[Turn over for Question 28(d)
on *Page twenty*

SECTION III

Marks

Part C—The Internet (continued)

28. (continued)

(*d*) Complete the HTML code missing from:

(i) line 11;

(ii) line 15.

2

[END OF SECTION III—PART C]

(50)

[END OF QUESTION PAPER]

[BLANK PAGE]

X216/301

NATIONAL QUALIFICATIONS 2008	MONDAY, 19 MAY 9.00 AM – 11.30AM	INFORMATION SYSTEMS HIGHER

Attempt **all** questions in Section I.

Attempt **all** questions in Section II.

Attempt **one** sub-section of Section III.

Part A	Applied Multimedia	Page 8	Questions 18 to 20
Part B	Expert Systems	Page 11	Questions 21 to 25
Part C	The Internet	Page 16	Questions 26 to 29

For the sub-section chosen, attempt **all** questions.

Read all questions carefully.

Do not write on the question paper.

Write as neatly as possible.

Marks

SECTION I

Attempt ALL questions in this section.

1. A shop's database has been created from data in un-normalised form. The diagram below shows 4 records from a table in the database.

Item Number	Item Description	Item Price	Supplier	Supplier Address	Supplier Telephone
12123	Canvas	£5·99	Fabriceeze	21 Castle Street	03214 665447
12234	Fine Brushes	£5·99	Colour Solutions	32 Fort Street	03118 876540
13224	Oil Paints	£35·99	Colour Solutions	32 Fort Street	03118 876540
23441	Spray Paints	£12·99	Colour Solutions	32 Fort Street	03118 876540

    (a) Choose a suitable primary key for this table. Give **one** reason for your choice.   2

    (b) Describe **one** problem with deleting an item from this table.   2

2. Explain what is meant by a *Boolean* data type.   2

3. Explain what is meant by *referential integrity* with regard to foreign keys.   3

4. State the *cardinality* of each of the following relationships.

    (a) Recording Artist and MP3 playlist   1

    (b) Hospital Ward and Patient   1

5. State **one** characteristic of data in first normal form.   2

6. State **one** reason why a *surrogate key* would be used in a table.   2

Marks

SECTION I (continued)

7. Explain the term *metadata*.

2

8. Below is a part of a statement given by a driver involved in a road accident:

"I was doing just under 30 miles per hour along High Road when the car skidded on the ice and hit the wall."

State the category of this information according to its

(*a*) *source* and

2

(*b*) *form*.

2

9. Explain the purpose of a *decision support system*.

2

10. State **two** areas of Web content covered by the Copyright, Designs and Patents Act 1988.

2

11. Ahmed has a problem using his project management software.

State **two** means by which Ahmed could obtain *user support* for this software.

2

12. Explain how online stores such as Amazon make use of *data mining* to promote sales.

3

(30)

[END OF SECTION I]

[Turn over

Marks

SECTION II

Attempt ALL questions in this section.

13. Northbank High School stores details of pupils' attainment.

An example is shown below.

Pupil Name	Tom Jones	**Pupil ID**	12132
Form Class	5C		
Form Teacher	Mr Lee	**Telephone**	143

Course Code	**Subject**	**Level**	**Grade**
5MAA1	Maths	Higher	C
FRC12	French	Intermediate 2	A
5EN12	English	Higher	B
SR11	RE	School-based	Ungraded
SP22	PE	School-based	Ungraded
DI332	PE	Higher	B

Details of Form Classes are also stored.

Form class	1A
Form teacher	Ms Simpson
Room	G13
Telephone	132

Form class	5C
Form teacher	Mr Lee
Room	A22
Telephone	143

Form class	3D
Form teacher	Mr Macgregor
Room	G14
Telephone	132

Form class	1D
Form teacher	Ms Mahdi
Room	D9
Telephone	261

This data can be represented in un-normalised form as

<u>Pupil ID</u>
Pupil name
Form class
Form teacher
Room
Telephone
Course code
Subject
Level
Grade

Using pupil ID as the primary key, transform this un-normalised data to third normal form.

You **must** show the intermediate stages of first normal and second normal form and identify all primary and foreign keys at each stage of normalisation.

17

SECTION II (continued)   *Marks*

14. Inverdon Insurance has several branches throughout the country, each with several salespersons. A sales recording system has been set up using a relational database. The data is held in the following tables.

Branch	**Customer**	**Sale**	**Salesperson**
Branch number	Customer number	Customer number*	Sales ID
Address	Customer name	Sales ID*	Sales name
Telephone number	Customer address	Date	Branch number*
	Customer telephone	Amount	

(a) Draw an *entity relationship diagram* to represent this data model.   **6**

Each month a report is produced to show the sales for each salesperson. The report for salesperson D Wilson for May is shown below:

Date	Customer	Amount
07/05/07	AcmeArtefacts	£450.00
08/05/07	Deco Designs	£250.00
15/05/07	Allied National	£1258.75
...	...	...
...	...	...
31/05/07	Logotek	£216.34
Total		**£5237.11**

(b) (i) Name the tables and fields which would be used to produce this report.   **5**

(ii) State **two** features of the RDBMS which would be used to calculate and display the total for this salesperson.   **2**

[Turn over

Marks

SECTION II (continued)

15. A monthly report is produced by several employees creating and editing sections of the document and then sending these to an editor over a Local Area Network.

    (a) (i) Name a suitable *topology* for this Local Area Network and draw a diagram of this topology.   **2**

    (ii) Describe how using a *stylesheet* ensures that the monthly reports conform to a house style.   **2**

    (iii) The monthly report contains charts. State which feature of the application software has been used to position the chart within the paragraph as shown below.   **2**

> Many questionnaires were collected to produce statistics to study the progress of our healthy eating campaign. The survey was carried out during the final week of March in each participating centre. The results make interesting reading and will be included in our submission for further funding. I have included a pie chart to illustrate the main points.
>
>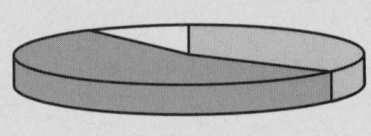

    (b) Examples of four different fonts used in the report are shown below.

    | Arial | Century | Tahoma | Times |

    Identify **two types** of font that are shown above.   **2**

    (c) (i) State the purpose of a *header* in a document.   **2**

    (ii) Describe how *pagination* could be used to improve the presentation of a multi-page document.   **2**

16. The ways in which shops and customers interact with each other have changed with the development of the Internet.

    (a) Describe **two** changes to the relationship between shops and customers brought about by the Internet.   **4**

    (b) Governments may block certain Internet content that they deem inappropriate. Describe **two** implications of this action.   **4**

17. Lachlan is preparing for an interview for the job of network security manager at First Place Ltd. The company has 4 warehouses supplying 40 branches throughout the country. A stock control system is used to manage daily supplies to each branch. As part of the interview he will be asked about a security strategy for the company's organisational information system.

    (a) State **five** areas concerning security strategies that Lachlan should be prepared to discuss in his interview.   **5**

    (b) Describe a suitable backup strategy for First Place Ltd. Your answer should describe:
    - a storage method
    - a recovery method
    - a rotation method.   **5**

    (60)

[END OF SECTION II]

SECTION III

Attempt ONE sub-section of Section III

Part A   Applied Multimedia   Page 8   Questions 18 to 20
Part B   Expert Systems   Page 11   Questions 21 to 25
Part C   The Internet   Page 16   Questions 26 to 29

For the sub-section chosen, attempt *all* questions.

[Turn over

SECTION III

Part A—Applied Multimedia

Attempt all questions.

Marks

18. A council has received funding to enable it to create a multimedia project providing information to members of the community about recent local developments. Community groups will be involved in the creation of a DVD-ROM to showcase developments in their own areas.

    (a) *Budget* and *timescale* are two items contained in a *contractual requirements specification.*

    State **three** other items found in a contractual requirements specification and give an example of each from the paragraph above.　　6

    (b) The World Wide Web was originally considered as a suitable delivery medium instead of a DVD-ROM.

    State **one** advantage and **one** disadvantage that a DVD-ROM has compared to the World Wide Web for showcasing recent local developments.　　2

    A sample screen from the DVD-ROM is shown below.

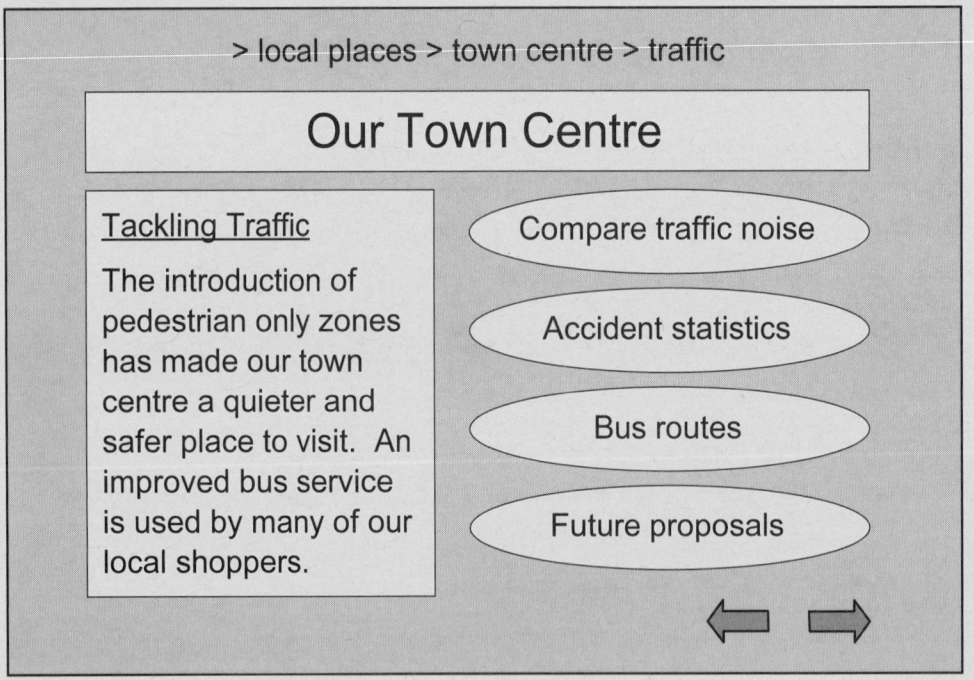

    (c) Identify and describe **two** methods that have been used in the sample screen to avoid users becoming "*lost in hyperspace*".　　6

    (d) Once completed, the product will be tested.

    (i) Describe the *screen testing* that would be carried out on the sample screen.　　2

    (ii) State **one** form of testing that would normally be carried out by persons outside the development team.　　1

    (e) MP3 and MIDI are two audio file types. An audio clip of traffic noise is to be included. State a suitable audio file type and justify your choice.　　3

Marks

SECTION III

Part A—Applied Multimedia (continued)

19. The home page for a school pupil's website is shown below.

(a) A metaphor has been used in the design of this site.

   (i) Explain what is meant by a *metaphor* in multimedia. 2

   (ii) Describe the metaphor used in this case. 2

(b) Wendy has included a scanned colour photograph on her home page. The photograph has been stored as a JPEG.

   (i) Give **one** reason for choosing JPEG as a file type rather than TIFF in this case. 2

   (ii) A GIF file type could also have been used, but this would have created a problem with *colour depth*.

   (A) A GIF file type has a lower colour depth than a JPEG. Describe **one** problem associated with using a lower colour depth to display photographs. 2

   (B) Dithering can be used to improve the appearance of images with a low colour depth. Explain what is meant by *dithering*. 2

(c) Describe how the homepage could be improved by the use of:

   (i) *kerning;* 2

   (ii) *anti-aliasing.* 2

Marks

SECTION III

Part A—Applied Multimedia (continued)

20. MecTrain is a company offering training to business users. It specialises in the use of multimedia for e-commerce. One of the training courses is based around a sample website selling a selection of jewellery. The website contains two sections: one where users can browse the catalogue of jewellery items and the other where users can make purchases online.

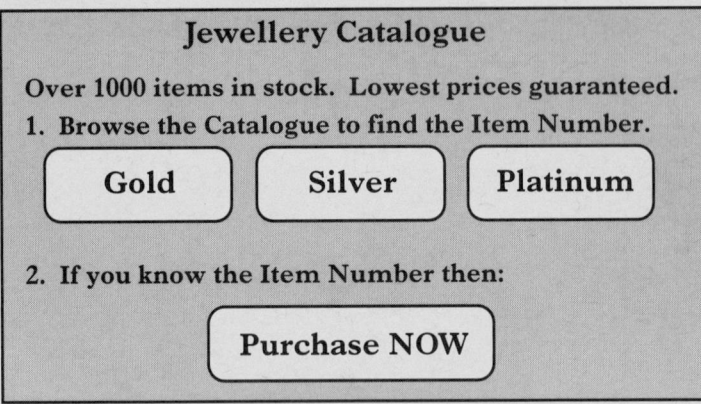

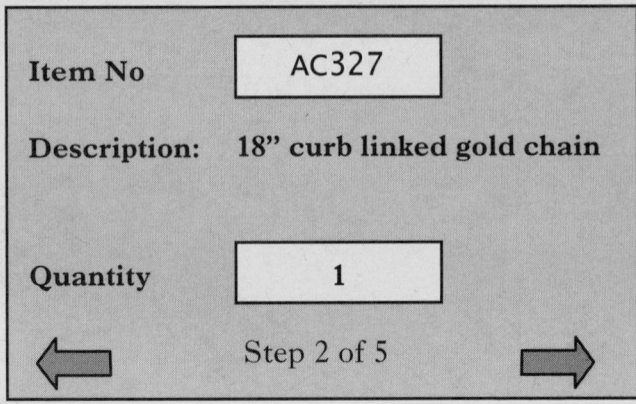

Figure 1: Screenshot of catalogue   Figure 2: Screenshot from on-line purchases

The diagrams above show a screen from the jewellery catalogue and a screen from the on-line purchases section, where the user enters the Item No and Quantity.

(a) State the type of user interface used in *Figure 2* shown above.   1

(b) The website uses a database to store details of its customers, jewellery items and orders. When a customer enters in the Item No the description automatically appears.

Explain how the description is retrieved from the database.   3

(c) The sample website uses a hybrid navigational structure.

   (i) Justify the choice of structure for this website.   4

   (ii) Draw a simple graphical representation of this structure.   3

(d) Describe how multimedia can be used to enhance *e-commerce*.   2

(e) Part of the training course focused on the use of *digital watermarks*.

   (i) What is a digital watermark?   1

   (ii) State the main purpose of using a digital watermark.   2

(50)

[END OF SECTION III—PART A]

Marks

SECTION III

Part B—Expert Systems

Attempt all questions.

21. MBV Car Repairs operates a number of garages in the UK. The company uses a car fault diagnostic expert system to identify faults with car engines.

    (*a*) Describe **two** benefits to MBV Car Repairs of the use of this expert system.   4

    (*b*) Describe **one** social implication of using this expert system.   2

    A customer brought in his sports car for repair. The engineers used the expert system to diagnose the problem with the car and, based on the advice given, they carried out the repair. However, the customer brought the car back the next day complaining that the car was still not operating correctly.

    (*c*) (i) State **two** stages of the development process of this expert system where an error could have occurred.   2

         (ii) For each stage in (*c*)(i) describe how the error could have occurred in this situation.   4

22. Expert systems are widely used in organisations along with other information systems.

    (*a*) Compare the use of expert systems within an organisation with that of a *management information system*, with reference to decision making.   4

    (*b*) Distinguish between an expert system and a relational database in terms of how data is represented.   4

[Turn over

SECTION III   *Marks*

Part B—Expert Systems (continued)

23. Colin and Sofie are fashion image consultants. They have been commissioned by an international jeans retailer to help construct an expert system. The expert system will advise customers on the style of jeans to buy.

The following rules represent advice on what type of jeans to buy if you have long legs:

> IF legs are long
> AND build IS regular
> AND wearing boots IS yes
> THEN advice IS to buy bootcut jeans.
>
> IF legs are long
> AND build IS regular
> AND wearing boots IS no
> THEN advice IS to buy square cut jeans.
>
> IF legs are long
> AND build IS slim
> AND wearing boots IS yes
> THEN advice IS to buy bootcut jeans.
>
> IF legs are long
> AND build IS slim
> AND wearing boots IS no
> THEN advice IS to buy slimfit jeans.

Here is the start of the *decision tree* to represent the rules above.

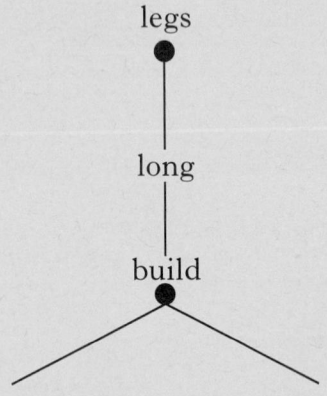

(a) Copy and complete the *decision tree* to represent the rules above   **6**

(b) Describe **one** advantage of using a decision tree to represent knowledge in an expert system.   **2**

(c) The expert system has to be expanded to cater for short leg lengths. Add to the list of rules to represent the following knowledge:

"The loose fit jeans are suitable for those with slim or regular build and suit the short leg length; they would not be worn with boots."   **4**

SECTION III

Marks

Part B—Expert Systems (continued)

24. Consider a *forward chaining* expert system containing the following rule base, where the letters G to R represent facts which are known or can be concluded.

    1   If G and H then P.
    2   If G then K.
    3   If H and J then L.
    4   If G and H and L then M.
    5   If H and N then R.

Suppose the working memory contains facts G, H and J added in that order.

  (*a*) (i)   List the rules that exist in the conflict set.   **3**

       (ii) Using *recency* conflict resolution strategy, state which rule would be fired first.   **2**

     (iii) Explain why conflict resolution strategies are required.   **2**

  (*b*) The following rule was added to the expert system. Represent this rule using propositional logic.

      If G and not L then N   **3**

[Turn over

SECTION III

Part B—Expert Systems (continued)

Marks

25. PHYSIO-24 is an expert system designed to diagnose sports injuries. Symptoms of the injury are requested from the user. The input is evaluated through a set of rules with certainty factors.

A simplified sample of rules for an injured foot is shown below.

> IF pain is on ball of foot
> AND bending toes is painful
> THEN patient is suffering from loss of padding on sole (0.7)

> IF pain is on heel
> AND pain is up leg
> THEN patient is suffering from damaged Achilles tendon (0.9)

> IF pain is on heel
> AND bending toes is painful
> THEN patient has heel spur (0.7)

The following facts are known with certainty factors given:

The pain is on ball of foot	0.5
Bending toes is painful	0.8
Pain is up leg	0.5
Pain is on heel	0.8

(a) (i) Calculate the certainty of the conclusion that the patient is suffering from loss of padding on sole. Show your working. **2**

(ii) Identify the conclusion drawn from the given facts. Explain your answer. **4**

(b) | "Severe pain and swelling on the ankle indicate that it is very likely that the ankle is broken." |

The following rule is added to the expert system to represent the knowledge above:

> IF pain is on ankle
> AND swelling is yes
> THEN patient is suffering from a broken ankle

State a certainty factor for this rule and explain your answer. **2**

(50)

[END OF SECTION III—PART B]

[Turn over for SECTION III Part C—The Internet on *Page sixteen*

SECTION III

Part C—The Internet

Attempt all questions.

Marks

26. Below is an extract from Northbank Sports Centre's home page with links to details of Gold Star, Silver Star and Junior memberships.

Northbank Sports Centre

Types of Membership	Description
Gold Star Member	Access all areas any time. Click for details
Silver Star Member	Off-peak access only. Click for details
Junior Member	Under 16 years of age. Click for details

The HTML code used to produce this extract is shown below.

```
1.  <h1>Northbank Sports Centre</h1>
2.  <table width="100%" border="1">
3.  <tr>
4.  <td>Types of Membership </td>
5.  <td>Description</td>
6.  </tr>
7.  <tr>
8.  <td><span style="font-family:Verdana">Gold Star</span>Member</td>
9.  <td>Access all areas any time.<a href="#Gmember">Click for details</a></td>
10. </tr>
11. <tr>
12. <td><span style="font-family:Verdana">Silver Star</span>Member</td>
13. <td>Off-peak access only.<a href="#Smember">Click for details</a></td>
14. </tr>
15. <tr>
16. <td><span style="font-family:Verdana">Junior</span>Member</td>
17. <td>Under 16 years of age.<a href="Juniormember.html">Click for details</a></td>
18. </tr>
19. </table>
```

(a) Explain the function of the width=100% attribute in line 2. **2**

(b) Explain the function of the <span> tag in rows 8, 12 and 16. **2**

(c) Rows 13 and 17 both use the href attribute of the <a> tag as shown below.

Line 13	href="#Smember"
Line 17	href="Juniormember.html"

Explain the difference in the way the href attribute is used in each of these lines. **4**

SECTION III   *Marks*

Part C—The Internet (continued)

26. **(continued)**

The club secretary does not like the look of the page and would prefer the designer to change to the layout shown below.

Northbank Sports Centre

Types of Membership   Description
Gold Star Member   Access all areas at any time. <u>Click for details</u>
Silver Star Member   Off-peak access only. <u>Click for details</u>
Junior Member   Under 16 years of age. <u>Click for details</u>

(d)   Rewrite the HTML code in each of the following lines to make the required changes.

    (i)   line 1   1
    (ii) line 2   2
    (iii) line 4   2

(e)   The updated web page is stored on the designer's computer. Describe how the designer would make this page available on the WWW.   3

27.   Donna is setting up her laptop as part of her home network. One of the configuration screens she has completed looks like this:

TCP/IP Settings

    Manual [X]   Automatic [ ]

IP Address   192.168.0.132

Subnet mask   255.255.255.0

Gateway address   192.168.0.1

(a)   TCP/IP is a set of communication protocols. Explain what is meant by a protocol.   2

(b)   Describe the function of each of the following protocols

    (i) TCP   2
    (ii) IP   2

(c)   The IP address 192.168.0.132 is a Class C address. Describe the difference between a Class A address and a Class C address in terms of the number of hosts and networks supported.   4

SECTION III   *Marks*

Part C—The Internet (continued)

28. Keith is developing a website for a friend's online computer store using php. Part of a page from the site which allows users to select items for purchase is shown below.

Click&Get.co.uk
File Edit View Favorites Tools Help
Back Forward Stop Refresh Home Search Favorites History Mail Print Edit
Address http://www.Click&Get.co.uk/ Go Links

Click&Get Online Computer Store   Today is: 26/5/08

Items meeting your requirements:

Item Number	Description	Number in Stock	Price	Add to Shopping Cart
CG1332	80GB External Drive more . . .	4	£65.99	☐
CG435	80GB Portable Hard Drive more . . .	1	£72.49	☐
CG212	120GB External Drive more . . .	12	£125.00	☐

Proceed to secure checkout

| Internet |

(a) (i) Why would *php* be a suitable means of producing this website?   4

    (ii) An image of the 120 GB External Drive is stored as CG212.jpg in a folder called images. State the URL which would be used to access this file.   4

(b) Describe the quality of the information shown above in terms of *level of detail*.   3

(c) Describe how the use of Secure Sockets Layer (SSL) ensures the security of data transmitted to the secure checkout area of the website.   3

(d) Click&Get makes use of *site usage tracking*.

    (i) Explain what is meant by site usage tracking.   2

    (ii) Describe **one** way in which Keith could implement site usage tracking on this website.   2

    (iii) Describe **one** use Click&Get could make of the information generated by site usage tracking.   2

SECTION III

Marks

Part C—The Internet (continued)

29. There are several organisations which contribute to the operation of the Internet. State which organisation would be most relevant in the following cases giving a reason for each answer.

   (*a*) A team of people developing a new web browser.

   2

   (*b*) An Internet Service Provider (ISP) wishing to greatly expand the number of users it can support.

   2

   (50)

[END OF SECTION III—PART C]

[END OF QUESTION PAPER]

[BLANK PAGE]

[BLANK PAGE]

[BLANK PAGE]

[BLANK PAGE]

[BLANK PAGE]